FHA Loans for Self-Employed, 1099 & Gig Workers

How Business Owners and Independent Contractors Qualify for FHA Home Loans

By Joseph G. Correa

Licensed Mortgage Broker, Finibi Mortgage

Copyright & Legal Notice

Published by Live Stronger Faster

First Edition, 2026

Table of Contents

Foreword

For millions of Americans, the traditional idea of employment no longer applies. The modern workforce has shifted dramatically, and today more people than ever earn their income through self-employment, contract work, freelancing, online businesses, commissions, and the gig economy. Entrepreneurs, consultants, real estate professionals, rideshare drivers, creatives, digital marketers, independent contractors, and small business owners now make up a powerful and growing segment of the economy. Yet despite earning strong and consistent income, many of these individuals are repeatedly told the same frustrating message when they try to buy or refinance a home: "You don't qualify." This book exists to challenge that belief and to show, clearly and truthfully, that self-employed borrowers are not shut out of homeownership—especially when FHA loans are used correctly.

The Federal Housing Administration loan program was created to expand access to homeownership, not restrict it. While many conventional loan programs rely on rigid income calculations and narrow definitions of employment, FHA guidelines were designed with flexibility in mind. They recognize that income does not always arrive in neat, predictable paychecks and that business owners often structure their finances differently for valid and legal reasons. Unfortunately, misinformation, outdated assumptions, and poor guidance have caused many self-employed borrowers to believe FHA loans are off-limits to them. This foreword—and the chapters that follow—are meant to reset that narrative and replace confusion with clarity.

One of the most common misunderstandings among self-employed and 1099 borrowers is the belief that FHA loans require perfect tax returns, high reported income, or W-2 employment. In reality, FHA underwriting focuses on stability, consistency, and the ability to repay—not on whether income comes from a traditional employer. Business owners are allowed to deduct expenses. Independent contractors are allowed to write off costs. Gig workers are allowed to have variable income. None of these facts automatically disqualify a borrower. What matters is how income is documented, analyzed, and presented within FHA guidelines. This book is designed to teach you exactly how that process works, so you can approach homeownership with confidence rather than uncertainty.

Self-employed borrowers face a unique challenge that salaried employees often never see: their income is scrutinized differently. Underwriters do not simply look at gross deposits or monthly averages; they analyze tax returns, profit and loss statements, trends, and the overall health of the business. For many borrowers, this process feels invasive or overly complicated, especially when they are unfamiliar with how lenders interpret business income. The goal of this book is to demystify that process. By understanding how FHA lenders evaluate self-employed income, you gain the power to prepare properly, avoid costly mistakes, and position yourself for approval before you ever submit an application.

Another reason this book is so important is that many self-employed borrowers unknowingly sabotage their own mortgage approval—not because they are unqualified, but because they receive incomplete or incorrect advice. Some are told to stop writing off expenses, which can create tax problems. Others are advised to delay buying for years unnecessarily. Still others apply with the wrong lender, the wrong loan program, or the wrong documentation, only to be denied and discouraged. FHA loans, when handled by knowledgeable professionals and informed borrowers, can be one of the most forgiving and effective paths to homeownership for self-employed individuals. This book exists to help you avoid misinformation and make smarter, more strategic decisions.

It is also important to understand that FHA loans are not just about buying a home—they are a powerful tool for long-term wealth building. Many self-employed borrowers think short-term, focusing only on whether they can get approved today. But FHA loans can be used strategically to purchase primary residences, multi-unit properties, fixer-uppers, and later to refinance, access equity, and reinvest in businesses or additional real estate. When used wisely, FHA loans can become a stepping stone not just to homeownership, but to financial stability and long-term growth. This book will help you see FHA financing not as a last resort, but as a strategic option.

The gig economy has changed how income is earned, but lending rules have not always kept pace with that change. Rideshare drivers, delivery drivers, content creators, influencers, online sellers, and app-based workers often earn income from multiple sources, platforms, and contracts. FHA guidelines allow for this complexity, but only when income is properly documented and averaged. This book will walk you through how FHA views gig income, what documentation is required, how long income must be received, and how to avoid common pitfalls that lead to unnecessary denials. Knowledge is the difference between being approved and being told to "come back later."

This book is also written with realism in mind. It does not promise shortcuts, loopholes, or guarantees. FHA loans still require documentation, verification, and responsible underwriting. However, what this book does provide is honesty. It explains what FHA truly requires, what lenders look for, and how self-employed borrowers can prepare themselves long before they apply. Preparation is the most overlooked advantage in mortgage lending, and for business owners, it can mean the difference between frustration and success.

Throughout this series, the focus has been on empowering borrowers with education rather than selling unrealistic expectations. Book 4 continues that mission by addressing one of the most underserved groups in the housing market. Self-employed borrowers are often financially savvy, disciplined, and entrepreneurial, yet they are frequently treated as high-risk simply because their income does not fit a traditional mold. FHA loans help level that playing field when borrowers understand the rules and work within them. This book gives you that understanding.

As you read this book, you will gain insight into how FHA calculates self-employed income, how tax returns are reviewed, how business losses are treated, how declining income is analyzed, and how compensating factors can strengthen an application. You will learn why two years of self-employment is important, what exceptions may exist, and how to explain your business story in a way that makes sense to an underwriter. These are not abstract concepts—they are practical tools that can be used immediately. This foreword is also an invitation. An invitation to stop assuming you are disqualified. An invitation to stop relying on hearsay or outdated advice. And most importantly, an invitation to take control of your homeownership journey as a self-employed borrower. FHA loans are not perfect, and they are not right for everyone, but they are far more flexible and powerful than most people realize. When used correctly, they open doors that many borrowers thought were permanently closed.

Book 4 fits into a larger vision of this series: to give borrowers the confidence to navigate FHA financing at every stage of life and income. Whether you are buying your first home, growing your business, rebuilding credit, or planning long-term wealth strategies, FHA loans can play a role. Self-employed borrowers deserve clear answers, realistic expectations, and practical guidance—and that is exactly what this book aims to deliver.

As you move forward into the chapters ahead, read with an open mind and a strategic perspective. This book is not just about qualifying for a loan; it is about understanding how lenders think, how FHA guidelines work, and how to align your financial story with a program designed to help people succeed. Self-employment should not be a barrier to homeownership. With the right knowledge, it can be a strength.

Welcome to Book 4 of *The FHA Homeownership & Wealth Series*. This is your guide to navigating FHA loans as a self-employed, 1099, or gig worker—and to proving that independence and homeownership can go hand in hand.

Chapter 1

Why Self-Employed Borrowers Think FHA Loans Are Impossible (and Why They're Wrong)

For many self-employed, 1099, and gig workers, the idea of qualifying for a home loan feels frustratingly out of reach. You may earn good money, run a profitable business, or consistently support your household, yet still hear the same discouraging response from lenders, real estate agents, or even friends: "Self-employed loans are hard," or worse, "You probably won't qualify." Over time, these repeated messages create a belief that FHA loans are designed only for W-2 employees with steady paychecks and simple tax returns. This belief is not only incorrect—it prevents many capable borrowers from ever attempting homeownership.

The truth is that FHA loans were never meant to exclude self-employed borrowers. In fact, the FHA program was created to expand access to housing, not restrict it to traditional employment structures. FHA underwriting guidelines recognize that income can come from many sources and that business owners often structure their finances differently for legal and strategic reasons. The problem is not the FHA program itself, but the widespread misunderstanding of how self-employed income is evaluated. Most borrowers are never taught how lenders actually read tax returns, calculate qualifying income, or determine stability for business owners.

One of the biggest reasons self-employed borrowers believe FHA loans are impossible is because their income does not "look" strong on paper at first glance. Business owners often deduct expenses to reduce taxable income, which is smart tax planning, but can create confusion during underwriting. Borrowers see a low adjusted gross income on their tax return and assume it automatically disqualifies them. In reality, FHA lenders look deeper. They analyze trends, business longevity, consistency, and net income over time. A single number on a tax return does not tell the full story, and FHA guidelines allow underwriters to consider that context.

Another major misconception comes from misinformation shared by lenders who may not specialize in FHA or self-employed borrowers. Some lenders focus heavily on conventional loans, which have stricter income requirements and less flexibility. When a self-employed borrower is declined for a conventional loan, they often assume FHA will be the same. This assumption is costly. FHA guidelines are more forgiving in areas such as credit history, debt ratios, and income variability, making them especially useful for entrepreneurs and gig workers when structured correctly.

Fear also plays a powerful role. Many self-employed borrowers fear that applying for a loan will result in rejection, wasted time, or damage to their credit. Others worry that lenders will scrutinize their finances too deeply or misunderstand how their business operates. These fears are understandable, but they often stem from a lack of education rather than actual risk. When borrowers understand what FHA lenders look for, they can prepare their documentation, strengthen their profile, and apply with confidence rather than anxiety.

Another reason FHA loans seem impossible is that self-employed income is not evaluated month by month. FHA lenders typically review two years of tax returns, averaging income and identifying trends. This long-term view can feel unfair to borrowers who have recently increased their earnings. However, it also protects borrowers from being judged solely on short-term fluctuations. Understanding this process allows borrowers to plan ahead, time their purchase strategically, and avoid applying before their income profile is ready.

Many self-employed borrowers also misunderstand the role of business losses. A loss on paper does not automatically mean financial instability. FHA lenders analyze whether losses are temporary, tied to startup costs, depreciation, or one-time expenses. They also examine whether the business is still generating cash flow. Too many borrowers assume a single bad year disqualifies them permanently, when in reality, FHA underwriting is designed to assess sustainability, not perfection.

The rise of the gig economy has added another layer of confusion. Borrowers who earn income from multiple platforms—rideshare apps, freelance marketplaces, online sales, or digital services—often believe their income is too fragmented to qualify. FHA guidelines allow multiple income sources as long as they are documented, consistent, and expected to continue. The problem is not complexity; the problem is clarity. Borrowers must understand how to document their income properly and present it in a way that aligns with FHA requirements.

Self-employed borrowers also tend to compare themselves unfairly to salaried employees. A W-2 worker may qualify with predictable income but limited flexibility. A business owner may have variable income but greater control, higher earning potential, and stronger long-term stability. FHA loans recognize this difference when underwritten correctly. The goal is not to fit self-employed borrowers into a W-2 box, but to evaluate them based on realistic and appropriate standards.

This chapter exists to dismantle the myth that FHA loans are out of reach for self-employed borrowers. The FHA program does not punish entrepreneurship. It simply requires documentation, consistency, and responsible financial behavior. Once borrowers understand the rules, they can stop guessing and start planning. Knowledge replaces fear, and preparation replaces frustration.

As you move through this book, you will learn how FHA calculates income, how underwriters think, and how self-employed borrowers can position themselves for success. FHA loans are not impossible for business owners. They are misunderstood. And when misunderstood programs are explained clearly, doors that once felt closed often open much faster than expected.

"The Numbers That Finally Made Sense"

Maria had been self-employed for six years, running a small digital marketing business from home. She earned income from multiple clients, invoiced monthly, and paid herself irregularly depending on cash flow. When she first tried to buy a home, she was told she didn't qualify because her tax returns "didn't show enough income." Discouraged, she gave up for two years, assuming homeownership wasn't realistic for someone like her.

In reality, Maria's business was profitable. In year one, her gross income was $95,000 with $45,000 in expenses, leaving $50,000 in net income. In year two, her gross income increased to $120,000 with $60,000 in expenses, leaving $60,000 in net income. However, Maria focused only on the expenses she deducted and assumed lenders would ignore her growth. She didn't realize FHA lenders average net income over two years and look at trends.

When Maria worked with an FHA-experienced lender, the math finally became clear. The lender took her net income from year one ($50,000) and year two ($60,000), added them together for a total of $110,000, and divided by 24 months. This resulted in a qualifying monthly income of approximately $4,583. Instead of seeing herself as "unqualified," Maria now had a clear monthly income figure that FHA underwriting could work with.

Next came the debt ratios. Maria had a car payment of $420 per month and student loans of $280 per month, totaling $700 in monthly debt. FHA allows higher debt-to-income ratios than many conventional loans. Using conservative guidelines, the lender calculated that Maria could spend roughly 43% of her $4,583 monthly income on total debts, which equaled about $1,971 per month. Subtracting her existing $700 in debts left approximately $1,271 available for a housing payment.

At first, Maria assumed $1,271 wouldn't be enough to buy a home. But FHA's lower down payment and flexible guidelines worked in her favor. With a modest purchase price, a competitive interest rate, and a small down payment, her estimated FHA mortgage payment—including principal, interest, taxes, insurance, and mortgage insurance—came to $1,240 per month. It fit within FHA guidelines with room to spare.

What shocked Maria most was that nothing about her business had changed. The only difference was understanding the math and how FHA lenders evaluated her income. She wasn't denied because she was self-employed; she was denied because no one had explained the rules correctly. Once the numbers were laid out logically, her path to homeownership became clear.

Maria closed on her home three months later. The same tax returns she once believed disqualified her became the foundation of her approval. The math didn't lie—she simply hadn't been shown how to read it. For the first time, Maria realized that self-employment wasn't a weakness in the mortgage process. When understood correctly, it was just another financial story that needed to be told properly.

Chapter 2

How FHA Lenders Really Calculate Self-Employed Income (Not What Most Borrowers Assume)

For self-employed, 1099, and gig workers, income is rarely as simple as a single number on a paycheck. Income rises and falls, expenses vary month to month, and tax strategies are often used to legally reduce taxable income. This complexity causes many borrowers to believe lenders will either misunderstand their finances or reject them outright. The reality is far more structured. FHA lenders follow a defined method to calculate self-employed income, and once borrowers understand that method, the process becomes predictable instead of intimidating.

FHA underwriting does not focus on gross revenue. It focuses on net income, trends, and stability. This distinction is critical. A business can generate large amounts of revenue but still show limited qualifying income after expenses. Conversely, a business with modest revenue but consistent profitability may be viewed favorably. FHA lenders begin by reviewing two full years of personal and business tax returns, looking for continuity of self-employment and income sustainability. This two-year requirement is not arbitrary; it allows lenders to identify patterns and reduce the risk of short-term income spikes or declines.

Once tax returns are reviewed, the lender identifies the borrower's net profit. For sole proprietors, this typically comes from Schedule C. For partnerships, it may come from K-1 forms. For corporations, it may involve additional analysis of distributions and ownership percentage. FHA lenders then assess whether the income is stable, increasing, or declining. Stable or increasing income is generally acceptable. Declining income does not automatically disqualify a borrower, but it does require explanation and careful analysis.

A common misunderstanding among self-employed borrowers is the belief that lenders average gross deposits from bank statements. FHA loans do not work that way. Bank statements may be used in limited circumstances to support income consistency, but qualifying income is derived from tax returns, not bank deposits. This is why borrowers who earn strong cash flow but aggressively deduct expenses sometimes feel penalized. FHA lenders are not judging tax strategies; they are assessing documented income. Understanding this distinction allows borrowers to plan their timing and documentation more effectively. After determining annual net income for each year, FHA lenders average that income over 24 months. For example, if a borrower earned $48,000 in year one and $60,000 in year two, the total of $108,000 is divided by 24 months to determine a qualifying monthly income of $4,500. This averaging smooths out fluctuations and provides a realistic representation of earning capacity. If income has increased significantly, lenders may use the most recent year alone, but this depends on documentation and underwriting discretion.

FHA lenders also evaluate whether income is likely to continue. This includes reviewing the nature of the business, industry stability, client concentration, and time in operation. A borrower who has been self-employed for several years in a stable industry may be viewed more favorably than someone newly self-employed with limited history. FHA guidelines allow for flexibility, but consistency remains the foundation of approval.

Business expenses receive particular attention during underwriting. Some expenses are considered non-cash, such as depreciation or amortization, and may be added back to income in certain situations. Others, such as vehicle expenses or home office deductions, are analyzed carefully. FHA lenders want to ensure that deductions do not mask an inability to repay the loan. Borrowers who understand how expenses are treated can better anticipate how their income will be calculated. Another critical factor is business ownership percentage. FHA lenders calculate income based on the borrower's share of the business. A 50 percent owner qualifies on 50 percent of net income. A 100 percent owner qualifies on the full amount. This seems obvious, yet many borrowers are surprised when income is reduced due to partial ownership. Clear documentation avoids confusion and delays.

Debt-to-income ratios are calculated after income is established. FHA allows higher ratios than many loan programs, but income must support the proposed housing payment and existing obligations. This is where understanding FHA math becomes empowering. Borrowers who know their qualifying income can estimate realistic price ranges before shopping for a home, avoiding disappointment and wasted time.

The most important takeaway from this chapter is that FHA income calculation is systematic, not subjective. It follows rules, formulas, and guidelines. Borrowers are not approved or denied based on opinion, but on documented numbers. When borrowers understand those numbers, they regain control of the process. FHA loans are not unpredictable; they are misunderstood.

This chapter sets the foundation for strategic planning. Once income calculation is clear, borrowers can decide when to apply, how to structure their finances, and what expectations are realistic. Knowledge transforms FHA underwriting from a mystery into a manageable process.

"Breaking Down the Math Behind the Approval"

Daniel was a self-employed electrician who operated his own contracting business. He had steady work, strong referrals, and more projects than he could handle. Yet when he first applied for a mortgage, he was told his income was "too complicated." The explanation ended there, leaving Daniel confused and frustrated. Determined to understand the process, he decided to break down the math himself.

Daniel reviewed his tax returns for the past two years. In year one, his Schedule C showed gross receipts of $140,000 with $90,000 in expenses, leaving $50,000 in net income. In year two, his gross receipts increased to $160,000 with $95,000 in expenses, leaving $65,000 in net income. Daniel initially focused on the $95,000 in expenses and assumed that lenders would see him as high-risk. What he didn't realize was that FHA lenders care most about net income and trends.

The FHA lender added Daniel's net income from both years: $50,000 plus $65,000, totaling $115,000. This amount was divided by 24 months, resulting in a qualifying monthly income of approximately $4,791. This number surprised Daniel. He had assumed his qualifying income would be much lower, but the math told a different story.

Next came Daniel's monthly debts. He had a truck payment of $520, a credit card minimum payment of $160, and a small personal loan with a payment of $220, totaling $900 per month. FHA guidelines allowed his total monthly debts to reach approximately 43 percent of his income, which equaled about $2,061. After subtracting his existing $900 in debts, Daniel had roughly $1,161 available for a housing payment.

Daniel initially worried that $1,161 would not be enough. But FHA's lower down payment and competitive interest rates made the numbers work. The lender structured a loan with a purchase price that resulted in a total monthly housing payment of $1,120, including mortgage insurance, taxes, and insurance. The loan fit squarely within FHA guidelines.

What changed for Daniel was not his income, business, or expenses—it was understanding the math. By seeing how FHA lenders calculated his income and debt ratios, he realized that the process was logical and consistent. The numbers weren't working against him; they were simply being misunderstood.

Daniel closed on his home within 45 days. What once felt like an impossible system became a clear formula. His experience proved that FHA loans are not designed to exclude self-employed borrowers—they are designed to measure risk accurately. When borrowers understand the math, the path to approval becomes far less intimidating and far more achievable.

Chapter 3

Documenting Income the Right Way—What FHA Underwriters Want to See and What Raises Red Flags

For self-employed, 1099, and gig workers, the biggest obstacle to FHA loan approval is rarely income itself—it is documentation. Many borrowers earn more than enough to qualify, yet their applications stall or fail because income is not presented in a way that FHA underwriters can clearly verify, analyze, and trust. Documentation is the bridge between what you earn in reality and what the lender can legally count on paper. When that bridge is built correctly, approval becomes far more likely.

FHA underwriters are not looking for perfection. They are looking for consistency, transparency, and reasonable explanations. The purpose of documentation is not to punish business owners for deductions or irregular cash flow, but to confirm that income is real, ongoing, and sufficient to support the loan. When documents are missing, incomplete, or contradictory, underwriters become cautious—not because the borrower is unqualified, but because the story does not align clearly. The foundation of FHA self-employed documentation begins with tax returns. Typically, lenders require two years of personal tax returns and any applicable business returns. These documents establish income history, business continuity, and ownership. Underwriters compare year-over-year figures to identify trends. Stable or increasing income strengthens an application, while declining income requires explanation. Borrowers often underestimate how closely underwriters read these documents, line by line, not just the bottom numbers.

Profit and loss statements play a critical supporting role. FHA lenders often require a year-to-date profit and loss statement to confirm that income is continuing at a similar pace. This document should align with tax returns and bank statements. When the profit and loss statement shows income far higher or lower than prior years without explanation, it raises red flags. Consistency between documents builds credibility, while mismatches invite scrutiny.

Bank statements are used to support—not replace—income documentation. FHA underwriters review bank statements to confirm that the business is active and generating revenue. Large unexplained deposits, inconsistent activity, or commingled personal and business funds can create delays. Borrowers who maintain separate business accounts and clean records make the underwriter's job easier and reduce the likelihood of additional conditions.

One of the most common red flags is unexplained declines in income. Declining income does not automatically disqualify a borrower, but it must be addressed. Underwriters want to understand why income decreased and whether the decline is temporary or ongoing. Clear explanations supported by documentation can resolve concerns. Silence, vague answers, or incomplete explanations almost always lead to stricter conditions or denial.

Another red flag is excessive deductions without context. While deductions are legal and common, underwriters want to ensure that deductions do not mask an inability to repay. Non-cash deductions such as depreciation may be added back in some cases, but cash expenses are treated differently. Borrowers who understand how deductions affect qualifying income can plan ahead and avoid surprises.

Ownership and control also matter. Underwriters verify ownership percentage, business structure, and decision-making authority. Borrowers who own a minority share may qualify only on their proportional income. Unclear ownership documentation creates risk from the lender's perspective. Clear operating agreements, partnership documents, and corporate records prevent unnecessary confusion. Consistency of work is another key factor. FHA underwriters want to see that the borrower's work is likely to continue. This includes reviewing the nature of the business, industry stability, and length of self-employment. A borrower who has been self-employed in the same field for several years is generally viewed as lower risk than someone who recently changed industries. Documentation should tell a logical story of stability.

The most important concept in this chapter is that documentation tells a story. Every document either supports or contradicts that story. When tax returns, profit and loss statements, and bank statements align, the story is clear and approval is easier. When documents conflict, underwriters slow down, ask more questions, and may ultimately decline the loan.

Self-employed borrowers often assume underwriters are looking for reasons to deny them. In reality, underwriters are looking for reasons to justify approval within FHA guidelines. Clear documentation gives them that justification. The better the documentation, the fewer assumptions underwriters must make—and assumptions are rarely favorable.

This chapter is not about overwhelming borrowers with

paperwork, but about empowering them to prepare intelligently. Knowing what FHA underwriters expect allows borrowers to organize documents, anticipate questions, and address concerns before they become problems. Documentation is not a barrier; it is a tool. When used correctly, it transforms self-employment from a perceived weakness into a well-supported financial profile.

"The File That Almost Fell Apart"

Kevin was a self-employed home renovation contractor with more than eight years of experience. His income was solid, his reputation was strong, and his workload was steady. Yet his FHA loan application nearly collapsed—not because of income, but because of documentation inconsistencies that raised red flags during underwriting.

Kevin's tax returns showed net income of $55,000 in year one and $58,000 in year two. The FHA lender averaged the two years, resulting in $113,000 divided by 24 months, or approximately $4,708 in qualifying monthly income. On paper, the numbers worked. Kevin's existing monthly debts totaled $820, leaving enough room for a housing payment under FHA guidelines.

The problem arose when Kevin submitted a year-to-date profit and loss statement showing significantly higher income. The

P&L indicated $75,000 in net income halfway through the year, which suggested an annualized income of $150,000—far higher than prior years. Without explanation, this raised concerns. Underwriters questioned whether the income was sustainable or overstated. Bank statements added another issue. Several large deposits appeared without clear descriptions, and Kevin had been using the same account for both business and personal expenses. While the deposits were legitimate, the lack of clarity forced the underwriter to request explanations and additional documentation. Each request delayed the process and increased the risk of denial.

Kevin worked with his lender to clarify the math. He explained that the higher income reflected a one-time commercial project and that his average income remained consistent with prior years. Supporting invoices showed the project's temporary nature. The lender adjusted the income calculation to rely on the two-year average rather than the inflated year-to-date figure.

With the corrected income of $4,708 per month, FHA guidelines allowed a maximum total debt of approximately $2,025. After subtracting Kevin's $820 in existing debts, he had about $1,205 available for housing. The lender structured the loan with a housing payment of $1,180, including taxes and insurance, which fit FHA requirements.

Once the documentation was clarified and aligned, the underwriter approved the loan. What nearly derailed Kevin's application was not income, but inconsistency. The math had always worked; the story had not been clearly told.

Kevin closed on his home weeks later, with a new appreciation for documentation. His experience demonstrated that FHA loans do not fail because borrowers are self-employed. They fail when the paperwork does not clearly support the numbers. When documentation tells a consistent, logical story, FHA underwriting becomes far more straightforward.

Chapter 4

The Two-Year Rule Isn't What You Think—How FHA Handles Time in Business, Exceptions, and Smart Timing

Few FHA rules intimidate self-employed borrowers more than the so-called "two-year rule." Many business owners hear this requirement and immediately assume they are disqualified if they have not been self-employed for exactly two full years. Others believe that even one month short of the two-year mark means an automatic denial. This misunderstanding causes many qualified borrowers to delay homeownership unnecessarily or never apply at all. In reality, the FHA two-year guideline is far more flexible and nuanced than most people realize.

The purpose of the two-year requirement is not to punish new entrepreneurs or gig workers. It exists to establish income stability and predictability. FHA lenders want to see that self-employed income is not temporary, speculative, or dependent on short-term circumstances. Two years provides a reliable data set to analyze trends, sustainability, and business viability. However, FHA guidelines allow for exceptions when the overall risk profile supports approval. Time in business is evaluated alongside work history. Borrowers who were previously employed in the same field before becoming self-employed may still meet FHA requirements with less than two full years of self-employment. For example, a W-2 employee who transitions into contract work within the same industry often demonstrates continuity rather than risk. FHA recognizes that the nature of income may change while the skill set and earning capacity remain consistent.

Another overlooked factor is how FHA measures time. FHA does not require borrowers to wait until the exact anniversary of self-employment to apply. Underwriters consider when income began, how it has been received, and whether it can be reasonably expected to continue. Borrowers who wait unnecessarily may miss favorable interest rates or housing opportunities based on incorrect assumptions.

Documentation plays a critical role when borrowers fall short of the two-year mark. Strong evidence of prior experience, contracts, recurring clients, and consistent earnings can support an exception. FHA underwriters are allowed to use judgment when guidelines are met in spirit, even if they are not met in a rigid calendar sense. This flexibility is often misunderstood or ignored by inexperienced lenders. The type of self-employment also matters. Some industries are inherently more stable than others. A licensed professional, consultant, or contractor with recurring clients may present lower risk than a startup dependent on a single customer. FHA underwriting evaluates the nature of the business, not just the length of time it has existed. Borrowers who understand this can better present their business story.

Strategic timing is another key consideration. Applying immediately after launching a business may not be ideal, even if income is strong. Conversely, waiting too long may not provide additional benefit once stability is established. FHA borrowers benefit from understanding when their income profile is strongest rather than applying based on arbitrary timelines.

Borrowers who experience interruptions—such as illness, family leave, or temporary closures—often assume their clock resets. FHA does not automatically restart the time-in-business requirement due to short interruptions. Context matters. Underwriters evaluate whether the interruption represents a permanent change or a temporary disruption. Clear documentation and explanations can preserve eligibility.

Another misconception is that FHA requires two profitable years. While profitability matters, FHA focuses on ability to repay. A borrower may have modest profits but strong cash flow and low debt. Others may show higher income but unstable operations. FHA underwriting balances these factors rather than relying on one rigid benchmark.

This chapter exists to shift self-employed borrowers from fear-based assumptions to strategy-based decisions. The two-year rule is not a wall; it is a guideline. When borrowers understand how FHA interprets time, continuity, and risk, they can make informed decisions about when and how to apply rather than waiting indefinitely.

The goal of FHA lending is sustainable homeownership. Time in business is one part of that equation, but it is never the only part. Borrowers who understand the full picture gain confidence, clarity, and control over their homeownership timeline.

"One Year, Ten Months, and the Numbers That Still Worked"

Luis left his W-2 sales job to start his own insurance brokerage. He had worked in the industry for over a decade, built strong relationships, and transitioned smoothly into self-employment. After one year and ten months in business, Luis assumed he needed to wait two full years before even considering an FHA loan. A rising housing market made him nervous, but misinformation kept him on the sidelines. When Luis finally spoke with an FHA-experienced lender, the math told a different story. His prior W-2 income averaged $70,000 annually. In his first year of self-employment, his net income was $62,000. In the partial second year, his year-to-date profit projected to $75,000 annually. The lender documented his prior industry experience and income continuity, allowing underwriting to proceed.

The lender averaged Luis's self-employed income conservatively. Using $62,000 for year one and a stabilized $70,000 for year two, the total of $132,000 was divided by 24 months, resulting in a qualifying monthly income of $5,500. This conservative approach satisfied FHA guidelines while accounting for his shorter self-employment history.

Luis's existing debts were minimal: a car payment of $410 and a credit card minimum of $140, totaling $550 per month. FHA guidelines allowed total monthly debt of approximately 43 percent of his income, or $2,365. After subtracting his existing debts, Luis had roughly $1,815 available for housing.

The FHA mortgage payment on the home Luis wanted—including principal, interest, taxes, insurance, and mortgage insurance—was calculated at $1,760 per month. Even under conservative assumptions, the numbers fit within FHA limits. The underwriter approved the loan with documented justification for continuity of income and industry experience. Luis closed on his home two months later. Had he waited for the exact two-year mark, home prices would have increased and interest rates would have risen. What made the difference was not bending rules, but understanding how FHA actually applies them.

Luis later admitted that the most expensive mistake he almost made was waiting based on bad advice. FHA did not require perfection or exact dates. It required logic, documentation, and reasonable math. Once those pieces aligned, approval followed naturally.

Chapter 5

The Hidden Power of Compensating Factors—How Self-Employed Borrowers Get Approved Even When the Numbers Are Tight

For self-employed, 1099, and gig workers, FHA approval is rarely determined by income alone. While income establishes the foundation of a loan file, the final decision often hinges on something far less discussed but incredibly powerful: compensating factors. These are strengths in a borrower's financial profile that offset perceived weaknesses such as lower income, higher debt ratios, recent business fluctuations, or limited time in self-employment. Understanding compensating factors transforms FHA lending from a rigid checklist into a balanced risk evaluation.

Many self-employed borrowers mistakenly believe that FHA underwriting is purely mathematical. They assume that if one number falls short, the loan automatically fails. In reality, FHA guidelines allow underwriters to consider the full financial picture. Compensating factors provide justification for approval when a borrower demonstrates responsibility, stability, and the ability to manage financial obligations despite irregular income patterns.

One of the strongest compensating factors is cash reserves. Reserves represent money left over after closing that can be used to make mortgage payments if income temporarily declines. FHA does not always require reserves, but when they are present, they significantly reduce risk. A borrower with three to six months of reserves demonstrates preparedness and financial discipline. For self-employed borrowers, reserves often carry more weight than they do for salaried employees because they show the ability to weather income fluctuations.

Low debt is another powerful offset. A borrower with modest income but very low monthly obligations may present less risk than someone earning more but carrying heavy debt. FHA underwriters look closely at total debt-to-income ratios, but they also consider how comfortably a borrower manages existing obligations. Self employed borrowers who avoid unnecessary debt strengthen their profile even if income varies year to year.

Credit history plays a critical role as well. FHA allows lower credit scores than many loan programs, but strong credit behavior still matters. A borrower with timely payments, limited delinquencies, and responsible credit usage demonstrates reliability. For self-employed borrowers, clean credit can offset concerns about income volatility. Credit history often tells underwriters more about repayment behavior than income alone.

Housing payment history is another overlooked compensating factor. Borrowers who have consistently paid rent or a prior mortgage at an amount equal to or greater than the proposed FHA payment show proven ability to manage housing costs. This factor is especially persuasive when income is tight. FHA underwriters view a strong housing payment history as real-world evidence that the borrower can handle the new obligation.

Length of self-employment and industry experience also serve as compensating factors. A borrower who has been self-employed for many years in the same field demonstrates resilience and adaptability. Even when income dips, long-term business experience reassures underwriters that the borrower understands their market and can recover. Stability often outweighs short-term fluctuations.

Another compensating factor is conservative loan structuring. Borrowers who choose lower purchase prices, higher down payments, or smaller loan amounts reduce risk. FHA underwriters view restraint favorably. Choosing a home that fits comfortably within budget, rather than stretching to the maximum limit, strengthens the case for approval.

Documentation quality itself can act as a compensating factor. Clean, organized, and consistent documentation reduces uncertainty. When underwriters do not have to guess, assume, or question, they are more likely to approve borderline files. Self-employed borrowers who proactively explain their financial story often succeed where others fail.

The most important lesson of this chapter is that FHA underwriting is not adversarial. Underwriters are not looking for reasons to deny loans; they are looking for ways to approve them responsibly. Compensating factors give underwriters the tools they need to justify approval within FHA guidelines. Borrowers who understand and strengthen these factors position themselves for success even when income is imperfect.

Compensating factors also empower borrowers to take control of their timeline. Instead of waiting indefinitely for higher income or perfect numbers, borrowers can focus on strengthening reserves, reducing debt, and improving credit. These actions often require less time and produce immediate benefits in underwriting.

For self-employed borrowers, FHA loans are not about fitting into a narrow mold. They are about demonstrating financial responsibility across multiple dimensions. When income, documentation, and compensating factors work together, approval becomes far more achievable than most borrowers expect.

"Approved Without Maxing Out the Numbers"

Tanya was a self-employed virtual assistant who worked with several long-term clients. Her income was steady but modest. Over the past two years, her net income averaged $48,000 annually, or $4,000 per month. Tanya assumed this income level would disqualify her from buying a home, especially in a competitive market. What she did not realize was how powerful her compensating factors were.

The FHA lender calculated Tanya's qualifying income at $4,000 per month. Using FHA guidelines, her maximum total monthly debt allowance at 43 percent came to approximately $1,720. Tanya's existing debts were minimal: a small car payment of $260 and a credit card minimum of $90, totaling $350 per month. This left approximately $1,370 available for housing.

Tanya's target FHA mortgage payment, including taxes, insurance, and mortgage insurance, was estimated at $1,420—slightly above the calculated comfort zone. At first glance, the numbers looked tight. However, the lender examined her compensating factors more closely. Tanya had no late payments on her credit report for over five years and maintained a credit score above 700. She also had $18,000 in savings after accounting for her down payment and closing costs, equaling more than six months of mortgage payments. Additionally, she had been paying $1,450 in rent consistently for three years without a single late payment. Her housing payment history alone demonstrated her ability to manage the new obligation.

The underwriter documented these compensating factors and approved the loan despite the tight ratios. The final FHA mortgage payment came in at $1,405—slightly lower than expected and well within Tanya's proven payment history.

Tanya closed on her home feeling empowered rather than stretched. She had not needed to earn more income or wait years to qualify. The approval was based on the full picture, not just one number.

Tanya later realized that her biggest obstacle had been assumption, not eligibility. FHA did not require her to be perfect. It required her to be prepared. By understanding compensating factors, she moved forward confidently and became a homeowner without overextending herself.

Chapter 6

One Paycheck, Five Platforms—How FHA Handles Multiple Income Streams and Gig Work

Modern self-employment rarely comes from a single source. Many self-employed and gig workers earn income from a combination of contracts, platforms, clients, and side businesses. Rideshare driving, freelance marketplaces, online stores, consulting work, digital products, commissions, and short-term contracts often coexist within the same financial profile. While this diversification can be a strength in real life, many borrowers fear it becomes a weakness during FHA underwriting. In truth, FHA guidelines allow multiple income streams—as long as they are documented, consistent, and likely to continue.

The first misconception borrowers have is that FHA prefers one clean income source. In reality, FHA underwriters care less about the number of income streams and more about their stability. Multiple income sources can actually reduce risk when they demonstrate diversification. A borrower who relies on several clients or platforms may be less vulnerable to losing income if one source disappears. FHA underwriting recognizes this when income streams are properly documented and analyzed.

The key requirement for any income stream is continuity. FHA generally requires a two-year history for self-employed income, including gig income, freelance work, and contract-based earnings. Underwriters review tax returns to confirm that income from each source has been received consistently. Income that appears sporadically or only once is usually excluded. Income that repeats year after year, even if variable, may be included.

FHA does not require each income stream to be equal in size. A primary income source may account for most earnings, while secondary streams supplement the total. Underwriters evaluate each source individually, then combine qualifying income into one monthly figure. This process prevents unstable income from inflating qualifying numbers while still recognizing legitimate earnings.

Gig workers often worry that platform-based income is treated differently. FHA does not disqualify income simply because it comes from an app or online platform. What matters is documentation. Tax returns, 1099 forms, and consistent reporting establish legitimacy. Borrowers who attempt to qualify based solely on deposits or screenshots without tax documentation often face challenges. FHA relies on reported income, not informal proof.

Another important consideration is overlap and timing. FHA underwriters want to see that multiple income streams coexist rather than replace one another. For example, if a borrower earned income from freelancing one year and switched entirely to rideshare work the next, underwriters may question continuity. However, if multiple streams operate simultaneously over time, they are more likely to be included.

Expenses associated with multiple income streams are also evaluated. Each business or platform may have its own deductions. Underwriters review net income after expenses rather than gross earnings. Borrowers sometimes assume that earning more from additional platforms automatically increases qualifying income, but if expenses rise proportionally, the net effect may be limited. Understanding this helps borrowers set realistic expectations.

Another common concern is workload sustainability. Underwriters assess whether a borrower can reasonably maintain multiple income streams without burnout or overextension. While FHA does not impose limits on hours worked, lenders consider whether income appears sustainable. A borrower working excessive hours across many platforms may be questioned, while a borrower with efficient systems and recurring clients may appear more stable.

Documentation clarity becomes even more important when multiple income streams are involved. Clean tax returns, organized schedules, and clear explanations prevent confusion. When underwriters struggle to identify income sources or reconcile numbers, they often exclude income rather than risk over-qualification. Borrowers who proactively explain their income structure reduce uncertainty.

This chapter exists to reassure borrowers that multiple income streams are not a liability. They are a reflection of modern work. FHA underwriting adapts to this reality when borrowers understand how income is evaluated. The goal is not to hide complexity, but to present it clearly and responsibly.

Multiple income streams can strengthen an FHA application when they demonstrate resilience, adaptability, and long-term earning potential. When borrowers understand how FHA combines income, they gain confidence and control over the process rather than fearing rejection based on misunderstanding.

"Five Streams, One Approval"

Marcus earned income from several sources. He worked as a freelance graphic designer, drove for a rideshare company on weekends, sold digital templates online, did occasional consulting projects, and earned affiliate income from a blog. While his total earnings were strong, Marcus assumed lenders would view his income as chaotic. For years, he delayed buying a home because he believed no loan program would understand his finances.

When Marcus applied for an FHA loan, the lender reviewed his tax returns carefully. In year one, his total net income across all sources was $58,000. In year two, it increased slightly to $62,000. While individual streams fluctuated, the overall trend was stable. The lender added both years together for a total of $120,000 and divided by 24 months, resulting in a qualifying monthly income of $5,000.

The lender then examined each income stream. Freelance design accounted for the largest portion and had been consistent for several years. Rideshare income appeared in both tax years and showed similar levels. Digital sales and affiliate income were smaller but recurring. Consulting income was occasional but repeated. Because each stream appeared consistently, all were included in the calculation. Marcus's monthly debts were modest: a car payment of $480 and student loans of $220, totaling $700 per month. FHA guidelines allowed total monthly debt of approximately $2,150. After subtracting existing debts, Marcus had roughly $1,450 available for housing.

The FHA mortgage payment on the home Marcus wanted was calculated at $1,390, including taxes, insurance, and mortgage insurance. Despite his complex income structure, the numbers fit comfortably within FHA limits.

What surprised Marcus most was that no income source had to stand alone. FHA did not isolate or penalize any single stream. It evaluated the full picture. The approval was based on combined, documented income rather than assumptions.

Marcus closed on his home knowing that his diversified income was not a weakness—it was a strength. The same complexity that once caused fear became proof of resilience. FHA did not require simplicity. It required clarity, consistency, and math that made sense.

Chapter 7

The Write-Off Trap—How Business Deductions Help You at Tax Time but Hurt You at Approval Time (and What FHA Actually Adds Back)

For self-employed borrowers, business write-offs are both a blessing and a curse. Deductions reduce taxable income, lower tax bills, and improve cash flow. Yet when it comes time to apply for an FHA loan, those same deductions can shrink qualifying income and make borrowers believe they are being penalized for smart tax planning. This chapter exists to clarify what FHA truly considers when reviewing deductions, what can be added back, and what will permanently reduce qualifying income.

The first misconception is that FHA disapproves of write-offs. FHA does not judge tax strategy. It simply relies on documented income to calculate repayment ability. Tax returns serve as legal proof of earnings, and deductions reduce the income FHA can count. This is not punishment; it is risk measurement. Understanding this distinction allows borrowers to plan rather than feel blindsided. Not all deductions are treated equally. FHA distinguishes between non-cash deductions and cash expenses. Non-cash deductions, such as depreciation and amortization, may be added back to income because they reduce taxable income without reducing actual cash flow. Cash expenses, on the other hand, represent real money spent and are generally not added back. This difference often determines whether a borrower qualifies.

Depreciation is the most common add-back for self-employed borrowers. Many businesses deduct depreciation for vehicles, equipment, or assets. Because depreciation does not require ongoing cash outflow, FHA lenders may add it back to net income when calculating qualifying income. This can significantly increase the borrower's monthly income on paper.

However, not all depreciation is automatically added back. Underwriters review whether the asset is essential to ongoing operations and whether replacement costs will be necessary. For example, depreciation on a delivery vehicle may be added back, but underwriters may still consider future replacement needs. FHA underwriting balances cash flow with sustainability.

Other non-cash deductions may include amortization, depletion, or one-time accounting adjustments. These are evaluated individually. Borrowers who understand which deductions qualify for add-backs can anticipate how income will be calculated rather than guessing. Cash expenses are treated differently. Advertising, supplies, insurance, rent, utilities, payroll, and meals represent real outflows. These expenses reduce available income and are not added back. Borrowers often assume that because these expenses are business-related, they should not affect mortgage qualification. FHA disagrees. The logic is simple: money spent cannot be used to make mortgage payments.

Vehicle expenses are a frequent source of confusion. Standard mileage deductions include both cash and non-cash components. FHA lenders analyze whether depreciation is embedded in mileage deductions and may limit add-backs accordingly. Clear documentation and explanations are critical in these cases.

Home office deductions also raise questions. While legal and common, they reduce qualifying income. FHA lenders generally do not add these back because they represent an allocation of real household expenses. Borrowers who rely heavily on home office deductions may see lower qualifying income.

The real danger is the write-off trap. Borrowers aggressively reduce taxable income without considering future mortgage plans, then feel trapped when qualification becomes difficult. FHA does not require borrowers to abandon tax efficiency, but timing matters. Strategic planning allows borrowers to balance tax savings with homeownership goals.

This chapter is not about advising borrowers to pay more taxes. It is about awareness. Knowing how write-offs affect FHA calculations allows borrowers to make informed decisions, adjust expectations, and plan their application timing strategically.

When borrowers understand what FHA adds back and what it does not, fear turns into strategy. The goal is not to eliminate deductions, but to understand their impact. Knowledge gives borrowers control long before underwriting begins.

"The $18,000 Add-Back That Changed Everything"

Eric was a self-employed photographer who specialized in weddings and commercial shoots. His business generated strong revenue, but his tax returns showed modest net income due to equipment purchases and vehicle deductions. When he first reviewed his tax returns, Eric assumed homeownership was out of reach.

In year one, Eric's gross income was $130,000. After expenses, his net income was $42,000. In year two, his gross income increased to $145,000, with net income of $48,000. At first glance, the two-year average net income of $45,000 suggested a qualifying monthly income of $3,750. Eric worried this would not be enough.

However, his lender examined his deductions more closely. Included in his expenses was $18,000 in depreciation related to camera equipment and a work vehicle. Because depreciation is a non-cash expense, FHA guidelines allowed it to be added back to income.

The lender recalculated Eric's income by adding the $18,000 depreciation back to his two-year net income total. The adjusted income became $108,000 over two years, divided by 24 months, resulting in a qualifying monthly income of $4,500. This adjustment alone increased his monthly income by $750.

Eric's monthly debts were minimal: a car payment of $390 and a credit card minimum of $110, totaling $500. FHA guidelines allowed total monthly debt of approximately $1,935. After subtracting existing debts, Eric had about $1,435 available for housing.

The FHA mortgage payment on the home Eric wanted, including taxes, insurance, and mortgage insurance, was calculated at $1,400 per month. With the depreciation add-back, the loan fit comfortably within FHA limits. Without it, approval would have been unlikely. Eric closed on his home knowing that nothing about his business had changed—only his understanding of the rules. The write-offs that once felt like barriers became manageable once he knew which ones FHA recognized.

Eric's experience proved a critical lesson: deductions are not the enemy, ignorance is. When borrowers understand how FHA evaluates write-offs, they can plan confidently and avoid unnecessary delays in their homeownership journey.

Chapter 8

From Application to Clear to Close—How Self-Employed Borrowers Survive Underwriting Without Losing the Deal

For self-employed, 1099, and gig workers, the most stressful part of the FHA loan process is often not qualifying—it is underwriting. Many borrowers are approved on paper, only to feel overwhelmed when the underwriter begins requesting documents, explanations, and clarifications. This phase can feel intrusive, confusing, and endless, especially for business owners with complex finances. Understanding how underwriting works transforms this stage from a source of fear into a manageable checklist.

Underwriting exists to confirm what has already been presented. FHA underwriters are not re-evaluating your worthiness as a borrower; they are verifying that the loan meets FHA guidelines and lender requirements. The more complex the income, the more documentation is needed. This is not a sign of trouble—it is a normal part of the process for self-employed borrowers.

The most common underwriting conditions relate to income verification. Underwriters may request updated profit and loss statements, additional bank statements, or explanations for variances between documents. These requests are meant to ensure that income remains consistent from application through closing. Borrowers who understand this purpose are less likely to panic when conditions appear.

Timing plays a crucial role during underwriting. Large deposits, unusual expenses, or major financial changes after application can trigger additional scrutiny. Self-employed borrowers who continue normal business activity without major financial shifts often experience smoother underwriting. Understanding what actions to avoid during this period—such as opening new credit, moving large sums without explanation, or changing business structure—reduces the risk of delays.

Another major source of conditions is business documentation. Underwriters may request operating agreements, letters from accountants, or confirmation of business continuity. These requests are not arbitrary. FHA guidelines require lenders to document ownership, control, and income stability. Borrowers who respond quickly and clearly keep the process moving forward.

Communication is one of the most powerful tools during underwriting. Borrowers who provide concise explanations rather than emotional responses help underwriters do their job. Underwriters are not adversaries; they are compliance professionals. Clear, factual responses supported by documentation are far more effective than frustration or resistance.

A common mistake is assuming that conditional approval means the loan is at risk. In reality, most FHA loans receive conditional approval. Conditions are simply tasks that must be completed before final approval. Understanding this normalizes the process and prevents unnecessary anxiety.

Clear to close occurs when all conditions are satisfied and the underwriter issues final approval. For self-employed borrowers, reaching this stage often feels like a victory. The complexity of income and documentation makes this milestone especially meaningful. Borrowers who prepare thoroughly often reach this stage faster than expected.

This chapter emphasizes preparation over reaction. Borrowers who anticipate underwriting requests can gather documents in advance, organize records, and respond efficiently. Preparation reduces stress, shortens timelines, and improves the overall experience.

Underwriting is not a test of patience; it is a process of verification. Self-employed borrowers who understand the rules, communicate effectively, and remain consistent are far more likely to reach the closing table without surprises.

"The Condition That Almost Cost Him the House"

Brian was a self-employed flooring installer who had been running his business for five years. His income qualified him comfortably for an FHA loan, and he received initial approval quickly. Confident the hardest part was over, Brian was unprepared for the underwriting phase.

Two weeks into underwriting, the underwriter issued several conditions. One condition requested updated bank statements. Another requested an explanation for a large deposit. Brian initially panicked, assuming the loan was falling apart. In reality, the deposit was a client payment he had received after application.

Brian worked with his lender to explain the math. His two-year average qualifying income was calculated at $5,200 per month. FHA guidelines allowed total monthly debt of approximately $2,236. Brian's existing debts totaled $760, leaving $1,476 available for housing. His FHA mortgage payment was $1,440—within guidelines.

The large deposit was $6,500 from a completed job. Brian provided an invoice and proof of deposit. The underwriter confirmed it was business income consistent with his tax returns and cleared the condition.

Another condition requested a year-to-date profit and loss statement. Brian's P&L showed income consistent with prior years, confirming stability. Once submitted, the underwriter issued clear to close.

Brian closed on his home on schedule. What nearly derailed the deal was not income or debt, but misunderstanding the underwriting process. The math had always worked. The conditions were simply steps to confirm it.

Brian later admitted that his stress came from fear, not facts. FHA underwriting was thorough, not hostile. Once he understood the process, the path to closing became clear.

Chapter 9

Timing Is Everything—When to Apply, When to Wait, and How Smart Self-Employed Borrowers Win the FHA Game

For self-employed borrowers, timing can matter just as much as income. Many qualified business owners are denied, delayed, or discouraged not because they lack the ability to repay, but because they apply at the wrong moment. FHA underwriting is heavily influenced by what the most recent documents show, and self-employed income tells a story over time. Applying when that story is unclear, incomplete, or temporarily weakened can make an otherwise strong borrower appear risky. Understanding timing allows borrowers to apply strategically rather than reactively.

One of the most common timing mistakes self-employed borrowers make is applying immediately after filing a tax return that shows lower income. Borrowers often assume that lenders will average income and smooth out the decline. While averaging does occur, FHA underwriters place significant weight on the most recent year when income is declining. This means that filing a return with aggressive deductions right before applying can reduce qualifying income at the worst possible moment.

Another critical timing issue involves incomplete tax years. Borrowers who apply early in the year may be required to provide year-to-date profit and loss statements. If income has not yet stabilized or ramped up for the year, those statements may weaken the file rather than strengthen it. Waiting until income trends are clearly established can make a substantial difference in underwriting outcomes.

Self-employed borrowers must also consider business cycles. Many industries are seasonal. Applying during a slow season may produce profit and loss statements that understate annual earning capacity. FHA underwriters do consider seasonality, but only when it is documented and consistent year over year. Borrowers who understand their business cycles can choose application windows that better reflect true income performance.

Another overlooked factor is expense timing. Large purchases, equipment upgrades, or one-time investments can temporarily inflate expenses and reduce net income. While these decisions may be smart for the business, they can negatively affect FHA qualification if they occur immediately before application. Timing major expenses after closing rather than before can preserve qualifying income without changing long-term tax strategy.

Credit timing also plays a role. Opening new credit accounts, increasing balances, or financing business equipment shortly before applying can raise debt ratios and create additional underwriting conditions. FHA allows flexibility, but underwriters evaluate current obligations. Self-employed borrowers benefit from maintaining stable credit behavior for several months before applying.

Cash flow timing matters as well. Borrowers who receive large deposits or irregular payments near application may trigger additional scrutiny. While legitimate, these transactions often require documentation and explanation. Applying during periods of predictable cash flow reduces complexity and speeds underwriting.

Another strategic consideration is interest rate environment. Waiting for "perfect" income numbers may cause borrowers to miss favorable rates or housing opportunities. FHA borrowers must balance income optimization with market conditions. Sometimes qualifying slightly lower but locking in a better rate produces a better long-term outcome than waiting indefinitely.

Timing also affects compensating factors. Borrowers who wait until they have built reserves, paid down debt, or established a strong housing payment history often strengthen their file significantly. These improvements may take months, not years, and can be more effective than chasing higher income alone.

The most successful self-employed FHA borrowers treat homeownership as a planned project rather than a spontaneous decision. They review tax returns in advance, analyze income trends, consult with knowledgeable lenders early, and choose application timing intentionally. This proactive approach prevents surprises and maximizes approval odds.

This chapter exists to shift borrowers from reactive to strategic thinking. FHA loans are not granted based on a single moment in time, but on patterns. When borrowers control when those patterns are evaluated, they gain a powerful advantage.

Timing does not require perfection. It requires awareness. Self-employed borrowers who understand when FHA looks most favorably at their profile can move forward confidently instead of waiting indefinitely or applying prematurely.

"Six Months Made a $400 Difference"

Nicole was a self-employed interior designer who earned strong income but struggled with timing. In the previous year, her net income was $68,000. Early the following year, she filed her tax return after taking significant deductions for software, marketing, and office upgrades. Excited to buy a home, she applied for an FHA loan immediately after filing.

The lender calculated her qualifying income using the most recent year. Her net income of $68,000 translated to approximately $5,667 per month. FHA guidelines allowed total monthly debt of about $2,437. Nicole's existing debts totaled $980, leaving roughly $1,457 available for housing. Unfortunately, the FHA mortgage payment on the home she wanted was $1,860. She was short by over $400.

Discouraged, Nicole assumed she needed to wait years. Instead, she worked with her lender to reassess timing. Over the next six months, her business income rebounded. Her year-to-date profit and loss statement showed consistent monthly income averaging $6,800. She also paid off a $240 monthly personal loan, reducing her debts.

When Nicole reapplied, the lender used a stabilized income approach. Averaging her prior year and current performance resulted in a qualifying income of approximately $6,300 per month. FHA guidelines now allowed total monthly debt of roughly $2,709. With her reduced debts of $740, Nicole had $1,969 available for housing.

The same FHA mortgage payment of $1,860 now fit comfortably within guidelines. Nothing dramatic had changed—no new career, no massive income increase. The difference was timing and preparation.

Nicole closed on her home shortly after. She later realized that applying six months earlier had cost her the deal, not because she was unqualified, but because the numbers were evaluated at the wrong moment. Timing turned a denial into an approval.

Her experience reinforced a simple truth: FHA loans reward preparation. For self-employed borrowers, when you apply can matter just as much as how much you earn.

Chapter 10

The Mistakes That Cost Self-Employed Borrowers Years—and the FHA Strategies That Actually Work

By the time self-employed borrowers reach this chapter, one truth should be clear: FHA loans are not impossible, unfair, or stacked against business owners. What derails most borrowers is not eligibility, but misinformation, poor planning, and costly mistakes repeated over and over by people who simply never learned the rules. This final chapter brings everything together by exposing the most damaging myths and mistakes—and replacing them with proven strategies that successful FHA borrowers actually use.

The first and most expensive mistake is assuming denial before applying. Many self-employed borrowers disqualify themselves mentally long before a lender ever reviews their file. They assume deductions ruined their chances, that gig income is unacceptable, or that they must wait years to qualify. This assumption delays homeownership, increases rent costs, and often results in higher future home prices and interest rates. FHA loans reward preparation, not self-doubt. Another common mistake is applying with the wrong lender. Not all lenders understand FHA self-employed guidelines equally. Borrowers often apply through banks or loan officers who specialize in conventional loans and treat FHA as a secondary option. These lenders may incorrectly deny applications, miscalculate income, or fail to use available flexibility. FHA loans require expertise. Choosing the wrong lender can cost a borrower months or years unnecessarily.

Timing mistakes also cost borrowers dearly. Filing tax returns with aggressive write-offs immediately before applying, making large purchases during underwriting, or applying during a temporary income dip can weaken an otherwise strong file. These are not fatal errors—but they are avoidable. Borrowers who plan their application timing gain a significant advantage.

Another major mistake is confusing gross income with qualifying income. Many self-employed borrowers focus on revenue, deposits, or invoices rather than net income and FHA calculations. This leads to unrealistic expectations and disappointment. FHA does not lend based on how busy you feel or how much money passes through your accounts. It lends based on documented, sustainable income. Borrowers who understand this stop guessing and start planning.

Documentation errors are another silent deal-killer. Inconsistent profit and loss statements, unexplained deposits, mismatched tax returns, or incomplete business records create doubt. Underwriters do not assume positive intent when information is unclear—they protect the lender and borrower by slowing down or declining the file. Clean, consistent documentation is not optional for self-employed borrowers. It is essential.

Many borrowers also misunderstand debt. They assume that income must increase dramatically to qualify, when in reality reducing debt often has a faster and more powerful impact. Paying off one loan, reducing credit balances, or avoiding new obligations can dramatically change FHA math. Smart borrowers work both sides of the equation.

Another costly mistake is waiting for perfection. Some self-employed borrowers wait for the "perfect year," the "perfect tax return," or the "perfect time." That moment rarely arrives. FHA loans are designed for real people with real financial lives. Waiting indefinitely often results in higher costs, missed opportunities, and frustration. Strategic readiness matters far more than perfection.

The most successful FHA self-employed borrowers follow a different approach. They consult early, review tax returns before filing, understand how income will be calculated, strengthen compensating factors, and choose timing intentionally. They treat homeownership as a project, not a gamble.

FHA loans reward borrowers who understand the rules and work within them. They do not require borrowers to abandon tax efficiency, hide income, or change careers. They require honesty, preparation, and realistic expectations. When borrowers adopt this mindset, FHA becomes one of the most powerful tools available to self-employed individuals.

This final chapter is meant to leave you with clarity rather than caution. FHA loans are not something to fear. They are something to use strategically. When you replace myths with math and assumptions with planning, the path to homeownership becomes far more achievable than most borrowers ever imagined.

"The Same Income, Two Different Outcomes"

Jason was a self-employed web developer earning solid income for several years. His net income averaged $72,000 annually, or $6,000 per month. Confident in his earnings, Jason applied for an FHA loan without preparation. He had just filed a tax return with heavy deductions, financed new computer equipment, and opened a new credit card for business expenses. The lender calculated his qualifying income at $6,000 per month. FHA guidelines allowed total monthly debt of approximately $2,580. Jason's debts included a car payment of $520, student loans of $340, equipment financing of $290, and credit card minimums totaling $230. His total monthly debt was $1,380, leaving $1,200 available for housing.

The FHA mortgage payment on the home Jason wanted was $1,750. The loan was denied. Jason assumed FHA loans simply did not work for self-employed borrowers.

Six months later, Jason tried again—but this time with a strategy. He paid off the equipment loan, reduced credit card balances, and avoided new credit. His debts dropped to $860 per month. His income remained the same, but his financial profile improved significantly.

Using the same $6,000 monthly income, FHA guidelines still allowed $2,580 in total debt. With only $860 in existing obligations, Jason now had $1,720 available for housing. The same FHA mortgage payment of $1,750 was still slightly high—but Jason also had six months of cash reserves and a strong housing payment history from years of rent payments at $1,800 per month.

The underwriter approved the loan using compensating factors. Jason closed on the same home that had once seemed out of reach. His income never changed. His understanding did. Jason's story highlights the central lesson of this book: FHA loans are not won by earning more money alone. They are won by understanding the system and positioning yourself correctly within it.

Chapter 11

Turning FHA into a Long-Term Strategy—How Self-Employed Borrowers Use One Loan to Build Stability, Equity, and Future Options

For many self-employed borrowers, the FHA loan is seen as a one-time solution—a way to finally get approved when other loan programs say no. While FHA certainly serves that purpose, limiting it to a single transaction misses its real power. FHA loans are not just an entry point into homeownership; they can be the foundation of a long-term strategy that supports stability, flexibility, and wealth-building for business owners whose income may change over time.

Self-employed income is rarely linear. Some years are stronger than others. Expenses fluctuate. Business priorities shift. FHA loans are uniquely suited to this reality because they emphasize sustainability rather than perfection. When used strategically, FHA financing can provide a stable housing payment while income grows, contracts, or evolves—something many self-employed borrowers underestimate when choosing loan programs. One of the most important strategic advantages of FHA loans is payment stability. Fixed-rate FHA loans offer predictable payments that allow business owners to plan confidently, even during slower income periods. This stability reduces financial stress and allows entrepreneurs to focus on growing their business rather than worrying about rising housing costs. For self-employed borrowers, predictable housing expenses are often more valuable than chasing the lowest possible rate.

Another overlooked benefit is FHA's role as a stepping stone. Many borrowers mistakenly believe FHA is a "last resort" loan. In reality, it is often a bridge. Self-employed borrowers can use FHA to buy a primary residence, build equity, stabilize income, improve credit, and later refinance into conventional financing if desired. FHA does not lock borrowers into permanent limitations; it creates options.

Equity growth is a critical part of this strategy. Even with mortgage insurance, FHA loans allow borrowers to begin building equity sooner than waiting years to qualify for conventional financing. Equity can later be accessed through refinancing, used to eliminate mortgage insurance, or leveraged for future investments. For business owners, equity represents optionality—capital that can support business expansion, emergency liquidity, or long-term wealth planning. FHA loans also support mobility. Life changes, businesses relocate, and opportunities arise. FHA's flexible guidelines allow borrowers to adapt. Whether refinancing, moving, or transitioning to another loan program, FHA does not trap borrowers. It provides a stable starting point from which decisions can be made thoughtfully rather than under pressure.

Another strategic benefit is FHA's compatibility with income growth. Many self-employed borrowers qualify with conservative income calculations early in their business journey. As income increases, FHA borrowers are not penalized for success. Improved income can support refinancing, removing mortgage insurance, shortening loan terms, or accessing better pricing. FHA accommodates growth rather than restricting it.

Risk management is another often-overlooked advantage. Self-employed borrowers face income uncertainty that salaried employees may not. FHA loans provide guardrails—reasonable qualification standards, stable payments, and flexibility during financial transitions. These features reduce the risk of overextension and foreclosure, making FHA a prudent choice for long-term financial health.

Some borrowers worry about mortgage insurance as a permanent burden. While FHA mortgage insurance can last longer than conventional PMI, it should be evaluated in context. Mortgage insurance is the cost of access—access to ownership, equity, and stability earlier than would otherwise be possible. When viewed strategically, this cost is often outweighed by the benefits gained.

The biggest mistake self-employed borrowers make is treating FHA as a temporary fix rather than a long-term tool. Borrowers who understand FHA's role in their broader financial plan make better decisions, experience less stress, and create more options for the future.

This chapter reframes FHA not as a compromise, but as a strategy. For self-employed borrowers, success is not defined by qualifying for the "best" loan immediately. It is defined by making smart decisions that support both personal stability and business growth over time.

FHA loans are not the end of the journey. They are often the beginning of one. When used intentionally, they provide the foundation upon which self-employed borrowers can build lasting security, flexibility, and wealth.

"The Loan That Bought Her Time"

Rachel was a self-employed wellness coach whose income fluctuated year to year. At the time she applied for an FHA loan, her two-year average net income was $54,000, or $4,500 per month. She knew her income was growing, but it had not yet reached a level that would qualify her for conventional financing.

Using FHA guidelines, Rachel's maximum total monthly debt allowance at 43 percent was approximately $1,935. Her only debt was a $310 car payment, leaving $1,625 available for housing. The FHA mortgage payment on a modest home she liked came to $1,580, including taxes, insurance, and mortgage insurance. The loan was approved.

Rachel viewed the FHA loan not as a limitation, but as a platform. Over the next three years, her business grew steadily. Her income increased to $78,000 annually. Her housing payment remained fixed, allowing her to reinvest profits into her business rather than chasing higher rent.

After three years, Rachel's home had appreciated and she had paid down her balance. Her loan-to-value ratio improved significantly. With higher income and increased equity, she refinanced into a conventional loan, removing mortgage insurance and reducing her interest rate.

The math told the full story. FHA had allowed Rachel to buy when her income supported $1,580 per month. Waiting for conventional approval would have required qualifying for a higher payment years earlier, during a more volatile income period. FHA bought her time—time to grow, stabilize, and strengthen her financial position.

Rachel later reflected that FHA had not been a fallback. It had been a strategy. The loan gave her stability when she needed it most and flexibility when she was ready for the next step.

Her experience demonstrated the true power of FHA for self-employed borrowers: not just approval, but progress.

Chapter 12

Buying with Confidence—How Self-Employed Borrowers Choose the Right Home Without Overstretching or Regret

For self-employed borrowers, qualifying for an FHA loan is only half the journey. The other half—often the more dangerous half—is choosing the right home. Many borrowers finally receive approval and feel pressure to buy immediately, stretch their budget, or chase the highest price they are "allowed" to purchase. This emotional shift can undo months or years of careful preparation. FHA loans are designed to support sustainable homeownership, not maximum leverage, and self-employed borrowers benefit the most when they understand how to choose a home that fits both their income and their lifestyle.

One of the biggest mistakes borrowers make is confusing approval limits with comfort limits. FHA underwriting calculates the maximum payment a borrower can theoretically handle based on guidelines and compensating factors. That number does not automatically reflect real-world comfort, especially for business owners with fluctuating income.

Self-employed borrowers must evaluate affordability not only on good months, but also on slow months. A home that feels manageable during peak income periods may become a source of stress during downturns.

Another critical consideration is total housing cost, not just the mortgage payment. FHA payments include principal, interest, taxes, insurance, and mortgage insurance. Property taxes can vary widely by location. Insurance costs can increase unexpectedly. HOA dues may rise over time. Self-employed borrowers who focus only on the loan amount often underestimate the long-term cost of ownership. FHA does not prevent borrowers from making this mistake—but education does.

Maintenance and repair costs also weigh more heavily on self-employed borrowers. Unlike renters, homeowners are responsible for unexpected expenses such as roof repairs, HVAC replacements, plumbing issues, and appliances. Business owners must plan for these costs alongside business expenses. Choosing a home that requires fewer immediate repairs or has predictable maintenance can preserve financial flexibility.

Location matters as much as price. A slightly less expensive home in a high-tax area may cost more monthly than a higher-priced home in a lower-tax area. FHA approval does not account for lifestyle costs such as commuting, utilities, or local insurance risks. Self-employed borrowers benefit from evaluating the full cost of ownership rather than focusing narrowly on purchase price.

Another overlooked factor is business adaptability. Many self-employed borrowers work from home, rely on flexible schedules, or expect business growth. A home that supports workspace needs, zoning flexibility, or future expansion can add long-term value beyond square footage. FHA borrowers should view their home not just as shelter, but as infrastructure supporting their livelihood.

Emotional pressure also plays a role. Competitive markets, bidding wars, and fear of missing out push borrowers to stretch. FHA borrowers must resist the temptation to treat approval as a finish line. Approval is permission to proceed thoughtfully—not a command to buy at any cost. Walking away from a deal that does not fit is often the smartest financial decision a self-employed borrower can make.

FHA loans provide flexibility, but they do not eliminate risk. Borrowers who choose conservatively often experience greater long-term satisfaction, less stress, and more financial resilience. A slightly smaller home with a stable payment often outperforms a larger home that consumes cash flow and limits business growth.

The most successful self-employed FHA borrowers approach home selection as a strategic decision, not an emotional one. They choose homes that allow room for income fluctuation, savings, and future opportunities. They treat the FHA loan as a tool for stability rather than a license for leverage.

This chapter exists to remind borrowers that the goal is not just to buy a home—it is to buy the right home. FHA loans support sustainable ownership when borrowers choose wisely. Confidence comes not from buying the most expensive home possible, but from knowing that the home you chose supports your life, your business, and your future.

"Approved for More Than He Should Have Bought"

Ethan was a self-employed videographer whose income averaged $84,000 per year, or $7,000 per month. His business was growing, and his FHA loan approval reflected that. Using FHA guidelines, his lender calculated a maximum total monthly debt allowance of approximately $3,010. Ethan's only existing debt was a $410 car payment, leaving about $2,600 available for housing.

At first, Ethan focused on that number. He began shopping for homes with FHA payments close to $2,550 per month. The homes were impressive, but something felt off. During slower months, Ethan's income dipped to $5,500. A $2,550 payment would consume nearly half of his income before business expenses.

Ethan paused and ran the math himself. He decided to base affordability on his conservative income months rather than his best ones. Using $5,500 per month as a baseline, he aimed to keep housing costs under $1,900. That number still fit FHA guidelines comfortably, but it was far below the maximum he was approved for.

Ethan chose a home with an FHA payment of $1,850, including taxes, insurance, and mortgage insurance. The purchase price was lower, but the home met his needs and required minimal repairs. He also maintained a healthy savings cushion after closing.

Six months later, Ethan experienced a slow business quarter. While other business owners around him felt squeezed, Ethan felt calm. His housing payment remained manageable, and he avoided dipping into savings or business credit.

Over time, Ethan's income continued to grow. Instead of feeling trapped by his mortgage, he felt supported by it. The math had worked not because FHA allowed him to borrow more, but because he chose to borrow less.

Ethan later realized that FHA approval had given him options, not obligations. The smartest decision he made was ignoring the maximum and choosing what made sense for his real life. His story illustrates the final lesson of this book: FHA loans work best when borrowers combine approval with discipline.

Chapter 13

Life Happens—How Self-Employed Borrowers Protect Their FHA Loan Through Income Swings, Emergencies, and Change

For self-employed borrowers, stability does not mean sameness. Businesses evolve, income rises and falls, industries change, and life events intervene without warning. Unlike salaried employees, business owners rarely experience straight lines. FHA loans are uniquely positioned to work within this reality, but only when borrowers understand how to protect their loan—and themselves—through inevitable changes. This chapter focuses on sustainability after closing, not just approval at closing.

Many borrowers believe that once they close on an FHA loan, the hardest part is over. In truth, the most important decisions often come after the keys are in hand. Self-employed borrowers must manage their mortgage alongside variable income, business expenses, taxes, and personal obligations. FHA loans are designed to support long term homeownership, but borrowers must actively protect that outcome through planning and discipline. The first principle of protection is payment prioritization. Housing payments must remain a top financial priority, even during slower business periods. Self-employed borrowers benefit from treating their mortgage payment as a fixed business expense rather than a flexible personal bill. This mindset shift helps ensure consistency and prevents short-term cash flow issues from becoming long-term housing problems.

Cash reserves play a critical role after closing. Many borrowers focus on reserves only as a compensating factor to qualify, then relax once the loan is approved. This is a mistake. Reserves are most valuable after closing, when unexpected expenses arise or income dips. FHA borrowers who maintain three to six months of housing payments in reserves significantly reduce the risk of missed payments during business slowdowns.

Income swings require proactive management. Self-employed borrowers should plan for their lowest-income months rather than their best ones. FHA loans do not adjust payments based on income, so borrowers must adjust their budgeting accordingly. Building buffers during strong months allows borrowers to coast through weaker periods without stress.

Another important consideration is tax planning after closing. While aggressive deductions can reduce taxable income, they also reduce cash flow if not planned carefully. Borrowers must balance tax efficiency with liquidity. FHA borrowers who work closely with tax professionals often maintain better cash flow stability while still minimizing tax liability.

Life events also impact self-employed borrowers more directly. Illness, family emergencies, market disruptions, or business pivots can reduce income suddenly. FHA loans include loss mitigation options such as forbearance and repayment plans, but these should be used strategically, not reactively. Understanding options before they are needed empowers borrowers to act calmly rather than from panic.

Insurance is another layer of protection often overlooked. Health insurance, disability insurance, and appropriate business coverage help ensure that income disruptions do not immediately translate into missed mortgage payments. FHA does not require these protections, but responsible borrowers view them as part of sustainable homeownership.

Another long-term consideration is adaptability. Self-employed borrowers may change business models, industries, or income sources over time. FHA loans do not restrict career changes, but borrowers must ensure that changes are made thoughtfully. Abrupt decisions without financial buffers can strain cash flow. Gradual transitions supported by reserves preserve stability.

The emotional side of homeownership also matters. Many self-employed borrowers carry stress differently than salaried workers. Financial uncertainty can amplify anxiety. Choosing conservative payments, maintaining reserves, and planning for variability reduces emotional pressure and improves quality of life. FHA loans support this approach by offering predictable payments and flexible options.

This chapter reinforces a core theme of this book: FHA loans are not about pushing borrowers to the edge of affordability. They are about creating a stable foundation from which self-employed individuals can live, work, and grow. Sustainability is not accidental; it is intentional.

Long-term success with an FHA loan does not depend on perfect income or flawless execution. It depends on preparation, flexibility, and the willingness to plan for uncertainty. Self-employed borrowers who adopt this mindset transform FHA from a loan program into a long-term support system.

"The Slow Season That Didn't Break the Mortgage"

Olivia was a self-employed wedding planner whose income varied significantly by season. Her two-year average income qualified her for an FHA loan with a monthly payment of $1,720, including taxes, insurance, and mortgage insurance. During peak months, Olivia earned over $8,000 per month. During slow months, her income dipped to around $4,500.

Before closing, Olivia made a deliberate decision to maintain six months of housing payments in savings. This amounted to just over $10,000. She also structured her business budget so that her mortgage payment was treated as a fixed cost, paid before discretionary business expenses.

Six months after closing, Olivia experienced an unusually slow season. Several events were postponed, and her monthly income dropped to $4,200. At first glance, the numbers looked concerning. But Olivia reviewed her budget calmly.

Her housing payment of $1,720 represented roughly 41 percent of her slow-month income. While tight, it was manageable. She used savings accumulated during strong months to supplement cash flow without missing a payment. Over a three-month slow period, she used $2,100 from reserves—well within her buffer.

When income rebounded, Olivia replenished her savings. Over the year, her total income remained consistent with prior averages. The FHA loan did not punish her for a temporary slowdown. It simply required consistency and planning on her part.

Looking back, Olivia realized that the loan itself had not been risky. The risk would have been ignoring seasonality and spending aggressively during high-income months. By planning for variability, she protected both her home and her peace of mind.

Her experience demonstrated that FHA loans do not require income certainty. They require income management. For self-employed borrowers, that difference is everything.

Chapter 14

The Self-Employed FHA Playbook—A Step-by-Step Roadmap from "Maybe Someday" to Confident Homeowner

For most self-employed borrowers, the biggest obstacle to homeownership is not income, credit, or even documentation. It is uncertainty. Not knowing when to apply, what to prepare, how lenders will evaluate their finances, or whether they are making the right decision at the right time creates hesitation that can last for years. This final chapter exists to replace uncertainty with a clear, repeatable playbook—a practical roadmap that self-employed, 1099, and gig workers can follow with confidence.

The FHA playbook begins with mindset. Self-employed borrowers must stop viewing FHA as a fallback option and start seeing it as a strategic tool. FHA loans are designed for real people with real financial lives, including variability, deductions, and growth curves. When borrowers accept that FHA is built for flexibility rather than perfection, they approach the process with clarity instead of fear.

Step one in the playbook is early self-assessment. Borrowers should review their last two years of tax returns before speaking to a lender. The goal is not to judge the numbers, but to understand them. What is the net income? Is it stable, increasing, or declining? Are there major deductions such as depreciation that may be added back? This self-awareness prevents surprises later and allows borrowers to plan strategically rather than react emotionally.

Step two is understanding qualifying income, not gross income. Borrowers must internalize that FHA uses documented net income averaged over time, not deposits or revenue. Once this is understood, borrowers can estimate realistic price ranges and avoid shopping beyond their comfort zone. This step alone saves months of frustration and disappointment.

Step three is optimizing timing. Self-employed borrowers should choose application windows intentionally. This may mean waiting until income stabilizes, delaying filing a tax return, or spacing out major business expenses. Timing does not require manipulation; it requires awareness. Applying at the right moment often matters more than earning a little more income.

Step four is strengthening compensating factors. Before applying, borrowers should focus on what they can control quickly: paying down debt, building reserves, maintaining clean credit, and documenting housing payment history. These factors often matter more than marginal income changes and can dramatically improve approval odds.

Step five is documentation readiness. Successful FHA borrowers treat documentation like a presentation, not a scramble. Clean profit and loss statements, organized bank records, clear explanations, and consistent numbers tell a coherent story. Borrowers who respect the documentation process reduce underwriting stress and move more smoothly to closing.

Step six is conservative home selection. FHA approval is not permission to overextend. Smart borrowers choose homes that fit their slowest months, not their best ones. This discipline protects cash flow, reduces stress, and allows business growth to continue without housing pressure.

Step seven is post-closing protection. The FHA playbook does not end at closing. Maintaining reserves, prioritizing housing payments, managing seasonality, and planning for life events ensure long-term success. FHA loans support sustainable ownership, but borrowers must actively manage variability.

The final step is long-term strategy. FHA loans create options. Borrowers can later refinance, remove mortgage insurance, leverage equity, or simply enjoy stable housing while income grows. The most successful borrowers think beyond the first transaction and use FHA as part of a broader financial plan.

This playbook is not theoretical. It reflects how FHA loans actually work in practice for self-employed borrowers who succeed. It replaces myths with math, fear with preparation, and hesitation with action. Borrowers who follow this roadmap rarely feel surprised by underwriting outcomes because they have already done the work.

The most important takeaway from this chapter—and from this entire book—is that FHA loans are not about fitting into a rigid box. They are about understanding the rules and positioning yourself intelligently within them. Self-employed borrowers who do this stop waiting for permission and start making progress.

Homeownership for self-employed borrowers is not a matter of luck. It is a matter of planning. The FHA playbook gives you that plan.

"From Freelancer to Homeowner—Following the Playbook"

Jordan was a self-employed content strategist who had worked independently for four years. His income fluctuated, but his two-year average net income was $66,000, or $5,500 per month. For years, Jordan assumed homeownership was a future goal, not a present option. After learning the FHA playbook, he decided to follow it step by step.

First, Jordan assessed his income honestly. His tax returns showed stable income with minor fluctuations. He identified $9,000 in depreciation related to business equipment that could be added back. His adjusted qualifying income became approximately $6,250 per month.

Next, Jordan calculated realistic affordability. FHA guidelines allowed total monthly debt of roughly $2,690. His existing debts included a $350 car payment and $180 in student loans, totaling $530. This left about $2,160 available for housing.

Rather than targeting the maximum, Jordan chose a conservative housing payment of $1,850, including taxes, insurance, and mortgage insurance. This payment fit comfortably within his slow-income months, which averaged $4,800.

Before applying, Jordan paid down credit cards, increasing his credit score and lowering monthly obligations. He also saved five months of housing payments in reserves, totaling just over $9,000. These compensating factors strengthened his file.

During underwriting, Jordan was prepared. He submitted a clean profit and loss statement, explained income fluctuations clearly, and avoided major financial changes. The loan moved smoothly to clear to close.

Six months after buying his home, Jordan experienced a slow quarter. His income dropped temporarily to $4,600 per month. Because his housing payment was conservative and his reserves intact, he made every payment comfortably without stress.

Two years later, Jordan's income increased significantly. He explored refinancing options and began planning long-term equity strategies. The FHA loan had not limited him—it had enabled him.

Jordan's experience proved the power of the playbook. He did not wait for perfect income or ideal conditions. He followed a process. The math worked because the strategy worked.

His journey closed the loop on everything this book teaches: FHA loans reward preparation, discipline, and understanding. For self-employed borrowers, that knowledge is the difference between "someday" and "done."

Chapter 15

Beyond the First Home—How Self-Employed Borrowers Use FHA as a Launchpad, Not a Limitation

For many self-employed borrowers, buying a home with an FHA loan feels like crossing a finish line. Years of uncertainty, misinformation, and hesitation finally give way to approval and ownership. But for borrowers who think strategically, FHA is not the end of the journey—it is the beginning. This chapter focuses on what comes next and how self-employed borrowers can use FHA as a launchpad for greater financial flexibility, stability, and opportunity rather than viewing it as a limiting loan choice.

One of the most important mindset shifts self-employed borrowers must make after closing is understanding that FHA is temporary by design, even if it lasts for several years. FHA loans are structured to provide access when income is variable or documentation is complex. As income stabilizes, credit improves, and equity grows, borrowers gain leverage. FHA gives borrowers time—time to grow their business, smooth income, and strengthen their financial profile without the pressure of rising rent or unstable housing costs. Equity accumulation is the first major advantage FHA borrowers gain after closing. Even with mortgage insurance, each payment builds ownership. Over time, appreciation and principal reduction work together to increase equity. For self-employed borrowers, equity represents optionality. It can be used to refinance, remove mortgage insurance, reduce interest rates, shorten loan terms, or create access to capital. Waiting years to qualify for conventional financing often delays this entire process.

Another powerful strategy is credit transformation. Many self-employed borrowers qualify for FHA with modest credit profiles. FHA's forgiving guidelines allow borrowers to establish a strong housing payment history, which often becomes the most influential tradeline on a credit report. On-time mortgage payments over 12 to 24 months can dramatically improve credit scores, opening doors to better financing options later.

FHA also provides flexibility during income growth. As businesses mature, income often increases unevenly. FHA does not penalize borrowers for success. Improved income strengthens refinancing options, allows for debt consolidation, or supports transitions into conventional loans with better terms. FHA acts as a stabilizer during growth rather than a constraint.

Some borrowers mistakenly believe they are "stuck" in FHA because of mortgage insurance. In reality, FHA mortgage insurance should be evaluated as a cost of access rather than a permanent burden. For many borrowers, the cost of waiting—higher home prices, higher rent, missed appreciation—far outweighs the cost of mortgage insurance. Strategic borrowers understand when it makes sense to refinance and when it makes sense to stay put.

Another overlooked advantage is optional mobility. FHA loans allow borrowers to adapt to life changes. While FHA loans are intended for primary residences, borrowers who later move for legitimate reasons may explore renting the property or transitioning to a new primary residence with different financing. FHA does not eliminate flexibility; it requires intent and compliance.

Self-employed borrowers must also think in terms of financial sequencing. FHA first, optimization second. Many borrowers reverse this order, waiting years to optimize income before buying. FHA allows borrowers to buy first, then optimize from a position of stability. This sequence often produces better outcomes, especially for business owners whose income trajectory is upward but uneven. Long-term planning also includes tax strategy evolution. Early in business growth, deductions may be aggressive. Over time, borrowers may shift toward income optimization rather than tax minimization, especially when preparing for refinancing. FHA borrowers who plan this evolution intentionally avoid surprises and missed opportunities.

The biggest mistake borrowers make after closing is complacency. FHA success does not require constant action, but it does reward awareness. Monitoring equity, credit, income trends, and market conditions allows borrowers to act when opportunities arise rather than reacting too late.

This chapter reframes FHA as a dynamic tool. It is not a box you are placed into; it is a platform you stand on. Self-employed borrowers who understand this stop asking, "How long am I stuck with FHA?" and start asking, "What does FHA allow me to do next?"

The answer, in most cases, is far more than they expected.

"The Three-Year FHA Advantage"

Caleb was a self-employed app developer whose income fluctuated significantly early in his career. When he applied for an FHA loan, his two-year average net income was $60,000, or $5,000 per month. Conventional lenders turned him away due to income variability, but FHA approval came through smoothly.

Using FHA guidelines, Caleb's maximum total monthly debt allowance was approximately $2,150. He had a $300 car payment and $200 in student loans, leaving $1,650 available for housing. He chose a conservative FHA mortgage payment of $1,580, including taxes, insurance, and mortgage insurance.

During the first year, Caleb's income increased modestly to $68,000. His housing payment remained fixed. In year two, his income jumped to $92,000. By year three, his income exceeded $120,000. Throughout this growth, his mortgage payment stayed the same, consuming a smaller and smaller percentage of his income.

Over three years, Caleb's home appreciated, and he paid down his loan balance. His loan-to-value ratio improved significantly. At the same time, his credit score increased due to perfect mortgage payment history. When he revisited financing options, the math told a powerful story.

With higher income, stronger credit, and increased equity, Caleb qualified for a conventional refinance. The new loan removed mortgage insurance and reduced his interest rate. His monthly payment dropped by over $400—even after refinancing costs were accounted for.

If Caleb had waited to buy until his income stabilized enough for conventional approval, he would have paid rent for three additional years, missed appreciation, and lost valuable time. FHA allowed him to buy early, grow safely, and transition later.

Caleb's experience demonstrated the long-term advantage of FHA for self-employed borrowers. The loan was not a compromise. It was a catalyst.

By using FHA as a starting point rather than a limitation, Caleb turned variability into leverage and uncertainty into opportunity. The math worked because the strategy worked.

Final Thoughts

From Uncertainty to Ownership—What This Book Was Really About

If there is one message that should stay with you after finishing this book, it is this: being self-employed does not make you a risky borrower—it makes you a misunderstood one. Throughout these chapters, you have seen that FHA loans were not designed to exclude entrepreneurs, freelancers, gig workers, or independent contractors. They were designed to include real people with real financial lives. The problem has never been the program. The problem has been the lack of clear, accurate information.

This book was written to replace guesswork with understanding. Too many self-employed borrowers spend years assuming they are "not ready," "not qualified," or "not the right type of borrower." Those assumptions are expensive. They lead to years of renting, missed appreciation, rising housing costs, and unnecessary stress. FHA loans exist to shorten that gap—to help capable borrowers move forward sooner, not later.

Another core theme of this book is control. Self-employed income may fluctuate, but the mortgage process does not have to feel chaotic. When you understand how FHA calculates income, evaluates risk, and applies flexibility, the process becomes predictable. Predictability restores confidence. Confidence allows you to plan instead of react. Planning is what turns homeownership from a dream into a decision.

This book also challenged the idea that approval is the ultimate goal. Approval is only a checkpoint. Sustainable ownership is the real destination. That is why so much attention was given to timing, home selection, cash reserves, compensating factors, and post-closing strategy. FHA loans are most powerful when they are used conservatively and intentionally, especially for borrowers whose income changes over time.

You have also seen that FHA loans are not static. They are adaptable. They allow you to buy when income is conservative, grow while payments stay stable, and transition when your financial profile strengthens. For self-employed borrowers, this adaptability is not a luxury—it is essential. FHA loans create breathing room during growth, which is something many traditional loan programs fail to provide.

Another important takeaway is that perfection is not required. Many borrowers wait for the "perfect year," the "perfect tax return," or the "perfect moment." That moment rarely arrives.

FHA loans were not built for perfect financial lives; they were built for responsible ones. Stable does not mean flawless. Qualified does not mean ideal. Understanding this frees you from unnecessary delay.

This book also emphasized something rarely discussed in mortgage conversations: emotional sustainability. Financial stress affects decision-making, health, and quality of life. Self-employed borrowers already carry more uncertainty than salaried workers. Choosing conservative payments, maintaining reserves, and planning for slow periods is not weakness—it is wisdom. FHA loans support this approach by offering predictable payments and reasonable guidelines.

Perhaps the most empowering lesson in this book is that income is only one part of the equation. Debt management, credit behavior, documentation quality, timing, and reserves often matter just as much, if not more. Many borrowers try to solve everything by earning more money when the faster solution is often reducing debt or improving structure. FHA underwriting looks at the full picture, and now, so do you.

This book was also meant to reframe how you see FHA itself. FHA is not a "lesser" loan. It is a different loan, designed for a different borrower profile. For self-employed individuals, that difference is often an advantage. FHA does not punish complexity—it requires clarity. When clarity is provided, FHA becomes one of the most forgiving and useful loan programs available.

If you take nothing else from these final thoughts, take this: you do not need to wait until your life looks like someone else's to buy a home. You do not need to fit a W-2 mold. You do not need to sacrifice entrepreneurship to gain stability. FHA loans exist precisely because not everyone's income fits neatly into a box.

The journey outlined in this book is not about rushing. It is about readiness. Readiness is not defined by a single number or milestone. It is defined by understanding where you are, what the rules are, and how to move forward responsibly. Once you have that understanding, fear loses its grip.

Homeownership for self-employed borrowers is not a gamble. It is a strategy. When you replace assumptions with math and hesitation with preparation, the process becomes far less intimidating and far more achievable.

This book was written so that fewer borrowers would say, "I wish I had known this sooner." Now you do know. What you do next is up to you—but at least you will be deciding from a place of clarity instead of confusion.

The FHA loan is not the end of the road. For many self-employed borrowers, it is the on-ramp. And with the knowledge you now have, you can choose when to merge—and where you want that road to take you.

The FHA Homeownership & Wealth Series

Complete Roadmap: From First-Time Buyer to Long-Term Wealth Builder

The FHA Homeownership & Wealth Series is designed as a progressive journey. Each book builds on the previous one, guiding borrowers from basic understanding to confident ownership, strategic financing, and long-term wealth creation. Readers can enter at any stage, but those who follow the full roadmap gain the clearest, fastest path to results.

This series is structured to meet borrowers exactly where they are—and show them what comes next.

Phase 1: Foundation & Confidence (Books 1–3)

Understanding FHA and realizing you qualify

These books eliminate confusion, fear, and misinformation. They are designed to answer the most important early question: *Is homeownership actually possible for me?*

Book 1 – FHA Loans Explained for Beginners How FHA Mortgages Work, Who Qualifies, and Why They're One of the Easiest Paths to Homeownership This is the foundation of the entire series. Readers learn how FHA loans work, why they exist, and how to evaluate FHA realistically using math instead of myths. This book builds confidence and replaces hesitation with clarity.

Book 2 – Buying Your First Home with FHA A Step-by-Step Guide to Purchasing a Home with Low Down Payment and Flexible Credit Rules This book turns understanding into action. Readers learn the full buying process—from pre-approval to closing—so they know exactly what to expect and how to avoid common first-time buyer mistakes.

Book 3 – FHA Loans for Borrowers with Low Credit or Past Credit Issues How to Get Approved with FHA Even with Late Payments, Collections, or a Low Credit Score This book is for borrowers who believe their credit disqualifies them. It explains FHA's second-chance philosophy and shows how recovery, not perfection, determines approval.

Phase 2: Income Reality & Property Flexibility (Books 4–6)

Qualifying with real-life finances and real homes

These books expand what readers believe is possible by addressing income types, property types, and cash requirements.

Book 4 – FHA Loans for Self-Employed, 1099 & Gig Workers How Business Owners and Independent

Contractors Qualify for FHA Home Loans This book demystifies income calculations for non-traditional earners and shows how FHA accommodates modern work patterns.

Book 5 – FHA Loans for Fixer-Uppers, Condos & Non-Perfect Homes How to Buy Homes That Need Repairs or Don't Fit Traditional Loan Guidelines Readers learn how FHA views property condition and how renovation and condo options expand buying opportunities.

Book 6 – FHA Loan Limits, Down Payment & Closing Costs How Much You Can Borrow and How to Bring Less Money to the Closing Table This book focuses on numbers. Readers learn how FHA loan limits work, how to reduce cash to close, and how seller credits and assistance programs change affordability.

Phase 3: Optimization & Refinancing Strategy (Books 7–8)

Using FHA beyond the purchase

These books show how FHA loans evolve with the borrower.

Book 7 – FHA Refinance Options Made Simple Streamline, Rate-and-Term, and Cash-Out Refinancing Explained for Homeowners Readers learn how FHA supports refinancing, payment reduction, and financial repositioning over time.

Book 8 – Using an FHA Cash-Out Refinance to Build Wealth How to Turn Home Equity into Cash Without Selling Your Home This book introduces equity as a strategic tool, not just a number on paper, while emphasizing responsible use.

Phase 4: Income & Expansion (Books 9–10)

Turning ownership into leverage

These books shift the reader from homeowner to strategist.

Book 9 – Buying Multi-Unit Homes with FHA How to Purchase 2–4 Unit Properties, Live in One, and Rent the Rest Readers learn how FHA enables owner-occupied investing and rent-offset strategies that dramatically reduce housing costs.

Book 10 – FHA Loan Myths, Mistakes & Borrower Strategies What Most Buyers Get Wrong—and How Smart Borrowers Win with FHA Loans This is the strategic wrap-up book that reinforces best practices, avoids costly errors, and helps readers think like informed borrowers.

About the Author

Joe Correa is a mortgage professional, educator, and financial strategist dedicated to helping everyday people understand homeownership, credit, and wealth-building without confusion or intimidation. With years of hands-on experience in the mortgage industry, Joe has worked with first-time buyers, self-employed borrowers, credit-challenged families, and aspiring investors who were often told "no" before learning what was actually possible.

What sets Joe apart is his ability to translate complex lending rules into clear, practical guidance. Rather than relying on theory, his work is grounded in real-world scenarios, real numbers, and real borrower outcomes. He believes that most people do not fail to buy homes because they lack income or discipline, but because they lack accurate information. His mission is to replace myths with math and fear with understanding.

Joe specializes in FHA loans because he has seen firsthand how transformative they can be when used correctly. He views FHA not as a last resort, but as one of the most powerful entry points into homeownership and long-term wealth—especially for borrowers navigating modern financial realities such as student loans, variable income, credit recovery, or limited savings. Through his writing, Joe teaches borrowers how to think strategically, act confidently, and use lending tools intentionally rather than emotionally.

In addition to his mortgage work, Joe is the creator of multiple educational programs and book series focused on homeownership, credit building, refinancing strategies, and financial independence. His approach emphasizes sustainability over speculation and progress over perfection. He is known for breaking down decisions into simple frameworks that empower readers to make smart choices at every stage of their journey.

Joe's writing style reflects his core belief: financial education should be accessible, practical, and empowering. He does not promise shortcuts or hype outcomes. Instead, he provides clarity, structure, and realistic paths forward—so readers can move from uncertainty to ownership with confidence.

When he is not writing or working with borrowers, Joe continues developing educational resources designed to help families build stability, equity, and long-term opportunity through informed financial decisions.

How to Get a Personalized FHA Review

If you found this book helpful, you may want to see how FHA loan options apply to your specific income, credit profile, cash to close, and homeownership goals.

Every borrower's situation is different. FHA guidelines, loan limits, interest rates, mortgage insurance, and available options vary based on income type, credit history, debt levels, savings, property type, and state guidelines. The examples in this book are educational, but your personal FHA eligibility, payment range, and strategy can only be determined through an individualized review.

As a licensed mortgage broker, I offer a **Personalized FHA Review** designed to show you: • Whether you currently qualify for an FHA loan • Your realistic home price and monthly payment range • How much cash you may need for down payment and closing costs • How credit, debt, or income factors affect your approval • Whether FHA is the best option for you now or later • What steps, if any, would strengthen your position

This review is fast, confidential, and focused entirely on helping you make informed homeownership decisions—without pressure or obligation.

To request your personalized FHA review, visit:https://finibimortgage.carrd.co/

You may also submit your information through the QR code provided in this book.

Your financial profile already tells a story.This review shows you how FHA lenders will read it.

Yours truly,

Joseph G. Correa

Licensed Mortgage Broker, Finibi Mortgage

Educational & Financial Disclaimer

This book is provided for educational and informational purposes only. The content is intended to help readers better understand FHA loans, homeownership concepts, and general mortgage strategies, but it does not constitute financial advice, legal advice, tax advice, or lending approval. Mortgage guidelines, FHA requirements, interest rates, loan programs, and qualification standards are subject to change and may vary based on individual circumstances, lender overlays, geographic location, and market conditions.

Nothing in this book should be interpreted as a guarantee of loan approval, loan terms, interest rates, or eligibility. All examples, scenarios, calculations, and illustrations are for educational purposes only and are not intended to represent actual loan offers or outcomes. Individual results will vary based on credit profile, income stability, debt obligations, assets, property characteristics, and lender-specific requirements.

Readers are encouraged to consult with a licensed mortgage professional, financial advisor, tax professional, or legal advisor before making any financial or real estate decisions. This book does not replace personalized advice or professional review. Any decisions made based on the information in this book are the sole responsibility of the reader.

The author and publisher are not responsible for any actions taken by readers as a result of the information provided in this book. While every effort has been made to ensure accuracy at the time of publication, no representation or warranty is made regarding the completeness, reliability, or current applicability of the information contained herein.

By reading this book, you acknowledge that homeownership and mortgage decisions involve risk and personal responsibility, and you agree that the author and publisher are not liable for any financial outcomes, losses, or damages that may result from reliance on this material.

This book is designed to educate, not to instruct or advise on individual financial decisions. Its purpose is to provide general understanding so readers can ask better questions, seek appropriate professional guidance, and make informed choices based on their unique circumstances.

Risk Disclosure

Homeownership and mortgage financing involve financial risk. While FHA loans are designed to increase access to homeownership and provide flexible qualification standards, they do not eliminate risk, and outcomes may vary based on individual circumstances, market conditions, and personal financial decisions. Purchasing or refinancing a home requires a long-term financial commitment and should be evaluated carefully.

Housing markets can fluctuate. Property values may increase or decrease over time, and there is no guarantee that a home will appreciate in value. Economic conditions, interest rate changes, local market factors, and unforeseen events can affect property values, mortgage payments, and resale opportunities. Borrowers should be prepared for the possibility that home values may remain flat or decline during certain periods.

Mortgage payments represent a fixed obligation that must be met regardless of changes in income, employment status, health, or personal circumstances. Failure to make mortgage payments may result in late fees, credit damage, default, or foreclosure. Borrowers should ensure they have adequate income stability, savings, and contingency planning before entering into any mortgage obligation. FHA loans include mortgage insurance, which increases the total cost of borrowing. While mortgage insurance enables access to lower down payments and more flexible credit standards, it may remain in place for a significant portion of the loan term unless refinanced or otherwise removed under applicable guidelines. Borrowers should understand how mortgage insurance affects monthly payments and long-term costs.

Refinancing, selling, or leveraging home equity is not guaranteed to be available in the future. These options depend on market conditions, interest rates, credit profile, equity levels, and lender requirements at the time of action. Borrowers should not assume future refinancing opportunities or equity access when making initial homeownership decisions.

Rental income, including income from multi-unit properties or converted rentals, is not guaranteed. Vacancies, maintenance costs, market conditions, tenant behavior, and regulatory changes can impact rental cash flow. Borrowers considering rental strategies should evaluate these risks carefully and avoid relying on projected rental income for financial stability.

This book does not provide investment advice or predict financial outcomes. All examples and scenarios are illustrative only and should not be relied upon as forecasts or guarantees.

Readers are responsible for conducting their own due diligence and seeking professional advice when appropriate.

By choosing to pursue homeownership or mortgage financing, readers acknowledge the presence of risk and accept responsibility for their financial decisions. The author and publisher are not responsible for any losses, damages, or adverse outcomes resulting from actions taken based on the information provided in this book.

This disclosure is intended to promote informed decision-making, not discourage homeownership. Understanding risk is a critical part of using FHA loans responsibly and sustainably.

www.ingramcontent.com/pod-product-compliance
Ingram Content Group UK Ltd.
Pitfield, Milton Keynes, MK11 3LW, UK
UKHW020158290926
15471UKWH00005B/944

9 798295 619915